Truth or

This by Tony Bradman

Illustrated by Chris Burke

FALKIRK COUNCIL
LIBRARY SUPPORT
FOR SCHOOLS

CAMBRIDGE
UNIVERSITY PRESS

Cambridge Reading

General Editors

Richard Brown and Kate Ruttle

Consultant Editor

Jean Glasberg

PUBLISHED BY THE PRESS SYNDICATE OF THE UNIVERSITY OF CAMBRIDGE
The Pitt Building, Trumpington Street, Cambridge CB2 1RP, United Kingdom

CAMBRIDGE UNIVERSITY PRESS
The Edinburgh Building, Cambridge CB2 2RU, United Kingdom
40 West 20th Street, New York, NY 10011-4211, USA
10 Stamford Road, Oakleigh, Melbourne 3166, Australia

Collection © Tony Bradman 1998
Illustrations © Chris Burke 1998
Cover photograph © Gerry Ball 1998

You're Late, Dad © Tony Bradman 1989; Spooked © Pat Moon 1998;
Life in the Back Row © Annie Fox 1998; That's the Name of the Game
© J. Burchett and S. Vogler 1995; Leopard © Richard Brown 1998;
The Tooth Person © J. Burchett and S. Vogler 1998; Threpperton via
Scadge © Dennis Hamley 1998

This book is in copyright. Subject to statutory exception and to the provisions of
relevant collective licensing agreements, no reproduction of any part may take
place without the written permission of Cambridge University Press.

First published 1998

Printed in the United Kingdom at the University Press, Cambridge

Typeset in Concorde

A catalogue record for this book is available from the British Library

ISBN 0 521 57552 4 paperback

Contents

You're Late, Dad

TONY BRADMAN

Steven's classroom was at the front of the school, and his desk was next to the window. So, just by turning his head slightly, he could see most of the street outside. It was almost lunch time, and they were supposed to be doing silent reading. But Steven couldn't concentrate on his book, even though it was a good one. He couldn't stop thinking about the afternoon. It was Sports Day and he knew, he just *knew* that he was going to win a race. And Dad had promised to be there.

Steven looked up. Mr Brooks was marking a huge pile of exercise books with a frown on his face. It was very quiet. All Steven could hear was the sound of Mr Brooks picking up exercise books and slapping them down again, and Samantha's wheezy breathing close behind him.

Samantha had broken her ankle, so she couldn't be in any races. But she sat next to Nicky, who was the fastest runner in the school, or so everyone said. He *was* fast, but Steven knew he was going to beat him today. He could see the end of the race in his mind, in slow motion, just the way it was on the TV.

He'd burst through the tape, Nicky miles behind him, and Dad would be right there, cheering him on. It was going to be great. No it wasn't . . . it was going to be amazing!

Out of the corner of his eye, Steven saw something moving in the street. He turned quickly, but carefully, so no-one would notice, and saw a car stop. But it was a red Metro, not Dad's dark blue Ford. It was too early for him to arrive yet, anyway. Sports Day didn't start till two o'clock.

Steven just hoped he wasn't going to be late this time.

Steven's dad looked at his watch and swore under his breath. It was nearly twelve . . . where had the morning gone? He'd got nothing done, even though he'd been frantically busy from the moment he'd sat down at his desk. The phone hadn't stopped ringing, so he hadn't even made a start on that report. And it was supposed to be finished today.

He did some quick mental arithmetic. If he started it now, he could probably finish it in an hour or so. It would take him five minutes to get to the car park, then half an hour to get to the school. He smiled to himself. There was plenty of time.

He pulled a pad towards him from the mess of papers on his desk, picked up his pen, and thought. A sentence began to form itself in his mind, but evaporated when the phone rang.

"Hello, Jim Morris speaking," he said.

"Hello, Jim, Bob Daniels here."

Jim sat up straight in his chair. Bob Daniels was his boss, and a very important man.

"Could you come over to my office for a meeting this afternoon, Jim? About three o'clock?"

Jim explained that he had already asked for the afternoon off to go to his son's Sports Day.

"Oh yes, I remember now . . ." said Bob Daniels. He paused. "That's a bit of a nuisance, Jim."

Jim knew the boss wasn't pleased about it. Bob Daniels liked his employees to do what *he* wanted, and show him what wonderful workers they were. He didn't think they should have time off for things like Sports Days.

"Can't your wife go instead?" he was saying. "This *is* very important."

"That's impossible, I'm afraid," said Jim curtly. He was cross now . . . Bob Daniels knew he was divorced.

"Well, pop in and see me before you go. I'd like a chat . . ."

Jim said he would, and put the phone down. He looked at his watch, then started writing very fast.

Steven picked at his food. He was too excited to eat, and besides, he didn't really like macaroni cheese.

7

He pushed his plate away.

"Are you leaving all that?" said Nicky, who was sitting opposite him. "I'll have it if you don't want it."

Steven said OK, and soon Nicky was scooping leftovers into his mouth as fast as he could go. Steven tried to concentrate on his yoghurt, but his eyes kept drifting back to the lumps of macaroni cheese disappearing into Nicky.

"Is your mum coming this afternoon?" Nicky said between mouthfuls. He didn't wait for an answer. "Mine is, and my dad said he'd be there too . . ."

Steven let Nicky's voice wash over him. Nicky's mum and dad would definitely be there, with his little brother, his baby sister, his granny and grandpa, an aunt or two, and even the dog, probably. His entire family always seemed to come to everything at the school, whatever it was, whenever it happened.

Steven's mum came to the school sometimes. She'd managed to get the afternoon off from her job for the Harvest Festival, and for the Christmas Concert. And when the headmistress had written to her about his school work, and how he needed to pull his socks up, she had come in to see her the very next morning.

But Steven's dad hadn't been to the school for years, not since before the divorce.

At first his mum wouldn't let him see Steven at all. Then they'd come to an agreement, and Dad was allowed to take him out on a Saturday. He was supposed to arrive at ten-thirty and bring Steven back at one o'clock. But he was always late. Most Saturdays, Steven spent ages standing at the window . . . waiting.

It hadn't mattered so much at first. Then Steven's mum got the job in the shop, and had to work on Saturday mornings. Dad was supposed to pick Steven up at nine-thirty now. She got really angry when he was late, as he was every week, without fail.

Last Saturday they had stood arguing in the street with Steven standing between them. He had closed his eyes and remembered all the nights he'd spent lying in bed, listening to his parents shout and fight downstairs.

He didn't miss all that. But he did miss Dad, although he never told Mum how he felt. She didn't like talking about Dad or the divorce, and Steven didn't want to upset her. They got on OK most of the time, and underneath it all she was still the same old Mum. But she was always so busy these days, and when she wasn't busy she was tired. And she hardly ever smiled.

Dad didn't do much smiling either. He lived in a pokey little flat on the other side of town, and

Steven knew he hated taking him there on a Saturday. That was why they spent most of their time together in the park, or at McDonald's, or driving out into the country to see the sights they'd seen a million times before.

When his mum told Dad how difficult it was to get an afternoon off for Sports Day, Steven's heart had sunk. There would be no-one there to cheer him on. And then Dad had said *he* would come. Steven had been amazed – and really, really pleased.

"I'll believe it when I see it," his mum had said as she'd marched off down the street to work. But his dad had promised.

"Don't you worry, son," he'd said. "I'll be there."

Nicky was eating an apple now, and still talking. Steven looked beyond him at the clock on the wall. It was one-twenty. He wondered where his dad was, right at that moment.

The lift wasn't working, so Jim ran down the stairs as fast as he could. By the time he got to the bottom, seven floors below his office, he was taking them three at a time. He swung round the banister at the end, and ran towards the main doors, nearly knocking the security man over as he shot out.

He was right in the middle of the shopping centre. Today it seemed as if everyone within a hundred miles had come in to shop. Jim could hardly get through the crowds. It usually only took him five minutes to reach the car park, but at this rate he'd be lucky if he ever got there at all.

He tried to run, dodging past the old-age pensioners, the mums with pushchairs, bumping into people and shouting sorry over his shoulder. It was a warm day and soon he could feel the sweat dripping off his forehead. His shirt stuck to his back and his suit jacket felt as if it weighed a ton.

It was Bob Daniels' fault that he was late. Jim had gone to see him on his way out, and had been treated to a little lecture about how his work had been suffering, how he needed to pull his socks up if he wanted to get on ... All he'd wanted to do by then was to get out, but you can't really hurry your boss when he's giving you a telling off. He'd just let the words wash over him in the end. He knew he wasn't doing his best at work, and he worried about it. Money had been really tight since the divorce, and it was getting harder just to make ends meet. The last thing he needed was to lose his job.

Barbara was right, though; it wasn't fair that she should be the one to go to Steven's school all the time. But she didn't seem to realise how difficult it was to explain things to a boss like Bob Daniels. It always ended in a row when they talked about it, and Steven hated them rowing. Sometimes he felt as if he was hardly part of Steven's life any more, but he didn't know what to do about it. Nothing was easy now. Everything was a mess.

Jim ran into the car park. His car was on the fifth floor, but the lift there wasn't working either, so he turned to go up the dark, dirty, graffiti-covered stairway. He stopped to get his breath back, and looked at his watch. It was one-thirty-three. He had a sudden vision of his son's face wearing a look of complete disappointment.

"I'll make it, Steven," he said aloud as he ran up the first flight. "I *swear* I'll make it."

"I don't think your dad's going to make it," said Nicky. Steven didn't say anything. He just kept his eyes fixed on the street beyond the fence round the school playing fields. He wasn't sure, but he thought his dad would have to come that way when he finally arrived. If he ever got there.

"He'll make it," he said.

"You can always come and stand with us while you wait," said Nicky. He waved in the direction of his family, a large group of people standing nearby. There were lots of small children with them, as well as several dogs, and they were all laughing and making a lot of noise. Steven didn't reply.

"Suit yourself," said Nicky. He walked off, and Steven watched him go. He wished now that he hadn't said anything about his dad coming, but it had all spilled out while they were getting changed. Nicky had been going on about his dad, and how he'd been a really great runner when he was the same age as them.

"My dad was a good runner too," Steven had said. And before he could stop himself, he was saying all sorts of things about his dad that weren't true, about how he'd been a brilliant runner and won loads of cups and medals. Nicky had looked as if he didn't believe him, which only made Steven want to say a whole lot more.

But now it was nearly two o'clock, and there was no sight of Dad anywhere. He was going to be late, that was for sure, but Steven had half expected that. It wouldn't matter so long as he got there before the big race, the four hundred metres, and that wasn't until two-thirty. So there was still time.

"Starters for the first race, please!" Mr Brooks called out. A gaggle of children surrounded him. "Not all at once, not all at once," he shouted crossly, and began handing out coloured bibs with numbers on them.

Steven looked towards the street again. "Come on, Dad," he whispered. "Where *are* you?"

Jim drummed his fingers on the steering wheel. The car in front hadn't moved for the last five minutes, and as far ahead as he could see there was a long line of cars, all well and truly stuck in a huge traffic jam.

He just couldn't believe it. It had taken him nearly ten minutes to get out of the car park, and another ten to get on to the bypass. Now here he was on what was supposed to be the fast route – and he wasn't moving at all.

He should have cut across town . . . it couldn't have been any slower. He daren't look at his watch. He knew he was late, and he didn't want to know *how* late any more.

Suddenly the car in front started moving, and soon the line of cars was edging slowly along. Jim sat up in his seat and tried to see what was happening. Four or five cars ahead, the line was slowing to a stop again. But just then, he saw an 'Exit' sign coming up on his left.

"Right," he said aloud. He sat back in his seat, swung the steering wheel over hard, and hit the accelerator. He shot away with a squeal of tyres, raced into the exit slip road and headed for town.

"Nothing's going to beat me today," he whispered as the engine roared. He was determined to make it. "Nothing . . ."

"Right," said Mr Brooks. "Starters for the four hundred metres, Class 5 boys. Come on, we haven't got all day!"

Steven and the others in the race took their numbered bibs from him. There were eight of them altogether, and Steven was number three, Nicky number two. So they'd be next to each other.

"Line up now," Mr Brooks was saying. Steven found his lane, and stood while the others found theirs.

"Come on, Nicky!" someone called from the crowd at the side of the track. Other voices joined in. "You can do it, Nicky! You can do it!" Nicky smiled and waved, then clasped his hands and raised them over his head like a champion.

Steven looked away, towards the street. There was no sign of a dark blue Ford, no sign of his dad. He wasn't going to make it. He wouldn't be there. He had broken his promise.

"To your marks please, boys," Mr Brooks said. The eight boys were now in their lanes, poised, waiting for the start. Steven looked down at the toe of his trainer on the white line just in front of him. He could hear a buzz of voices, then everything seemed to go quiet. His throat felt tight and his eyes were prickling.

A tear ran down his cheek and fell on a white-painted blade of grass. It made the white run.

"Ready . . . steady . . ."

There was a bang, and Steven was running.

Jim swung the car round the corner and squealed to a halt in the first space he could see. One of the front wheels hit the kerb with a clunk, and he knew without looking that the back of the car was sticking well out into the road. But he didn't care.

He flung open the door, jumped out and started running past the school fence. He could hear a crowd cheering and calling names, and as he looked he could see some children running round the track on the playing fields.

He came to the school gates at last, and ran through. He didn't stop, but ran straight on, past the main building, past the playground, past the infants sitting in a group with their teachers, past the headmistress and the head of the board of governors who both stared at him open-mouthed, and right up to the winning line . . .

. . . Just as two boys came off the last bend and headed for the tape. They were neck and neck, each straining to get in front of the other.

Steven could feel Nicky right next to him. He could hear voices calling Nicky's name, he could feel his legs getting tired, his heart beating as if it was going to explode, his lungs bursting. He wasn't going to make it.

"Come on, Steven!" Someone was calling out *his* name. "Come on, Steven, you can do it!"

There wasn't far to go now. Steven could see the tape, and standing beyond it he could see his dad. He ran, he ran as fast as he could. He burst through the tape and into his dad's arms.

At first neither of them could speak. They were both out of breath, puffing and panting and holding on to each other. Out of the corner of his eye, Steven could see Nicky's mum and dad walking off with him, their arms round his shoulders. Nicky looked back at him, but Steven didn't care about anything or anyone else.

He freed a hand to wipe his eyes, then stepped back and looked up at his dad.

"Steven, I . . ." Jim started to say.

"You're late, Dad," said Steven, but he smiled as he said it. His dad smiled back, then put an arm round Steven's shoulder. They walked off together towards the others.

Spooked

PAT MOON

"I don't believe in ghosts."

That's what Ali said.

"It's all imagination," he went on. "Imagination makes people see things that aren't there. You'd know that – if you had a scientific mind, like me."

He said it that night we were camped out in my back garden. He doesn't say it now though. Not after what happened. But that came later.

There was Ali, Shaun and me in the tent. We were trying to spook each other in the dark. Shaun was telling us this ghost story his brother had told him.

"This ghost has no face, see," he began. "It wanders the earth searching for a face. If it catches you, it takes *your* face, and your body too. It gets you when you're sleeping – just lies down on you and takes you over. It takes six hours. If you wake up before six hours, you're safe. If not, when you get up, there you are – a ghost without a face. You look down and there's *your* body in the bed. It looks exactly like you. Only it isn't. The ghost has got it now. It takes over your life. And you become the faceless ghost, searching for someone else to take over."

"How would you know the body looked like you?" asked Ali. "You wouldn't be able to see it, would you? Not without a face."

"This ghost can," said Shaun.

"Shh!" hushed Ali. "There's something outside."

We crouched in the dark, listening. I could hear it too. Soft swishing noises.

"Yeah, Ali. Very funny," I muttered. Ali likes winding people up.

"It's not me – it's the faceless ghost," he breathed spookily.

"Just put the torch on, will you?" Shaun croaked.

Whatever it was, it was getting closer. The noises stopped. Right outside the tent.

Ali flicked on his torch. "Look! It's trying to get in."

He was right. The tent zip was slowly opening. So was Shaun's mouth. I'd stopped breathing. I could see pale, bony fingers slide through the opening . . . and the white blob of a face . . .

"All right in there, then?" said my dad.

My breath gushed out with relief. So did Shaun's.

"Your mum and I are off to bed now, Kenny," Dad said. "We'll leave the back door unlocked and the kitchen light on, OK?"

"We're not little kids, Dad."

"Ha! You should have seen your faces!" laughed Ali when Dad had gone. "You really thought it was a ghost, didn't you? You were well spooked!"

"Nah," shrugged Shaun, not very convincingly.

"Good," joked Ali. "You won't mind sleeping at the zip end. Just in case."

"Yeah," I said. "You can be the ghost alarm. It'll get you first. We'll hear you screaming and it'll give us time to escape."

We crawled into our sleeping bags.

"Anyway," sneered Shaun, "it wouldn't need to undo a zip, would it? Ghosts can pass through anything. It'll probably get you first."

I couldn't get to sleep. Neither could Shaun. I could hear his fidgeting and his breathing. It wasn't the sleeping sort. Ali had gone straight off. But my imagination had gone into overdrive. Perhaps the faceless ghost had slipped inside the tent. Perhaps those noises were Shaun struggling . . .

"Oi, Shaun!" I whispered.

"Yeah?"

"Nothing."

Next morning, when we were sitting on our sleeping bags eating our Frosties, Ali said, "Here, Shaun. What's our teacher's name?"

"What?"

"Our teacher's name – what is it?"

Shaun frowned. He knew it was a trick question.

"He doesn't know, Ali," I joked. " 'Cos he's not Shaun any more. The faceless ghost got Shaun during the night. This kid looks the same, but it's not really him."

"Mrs Catchpole," Shaun blurted.

"Who's Mrs Catchpole? We don't know any Mrs Catchpole, do we Kenny?" Ali grinned.

"Poor old Shaun. Wandering the earth. Faceless," I said.

"Just shut up, will you?" Shaun yelled. He left after that. Said he had to clean out his gerbils.

"Me, I'd love to see a ghost," said Ali. "It'd be really interesting."

"Thought you didn't believe in them."

"I don't. It's all stories. As soon as someone checks a story out – *scientifically* – nothing. Zero. Zilch. But I'd love the chance to follow up a ghost story myself and prove it."

Then a big grin spread across his face. "Kenny, I've got an idea." He jumped up. "Come on!"

"Like what sort of idea?"

"Like a spook hunt."

"Oh yeah, Ali. Brilliant! Plenty of them on a sunny day in Fenton."

"Trust me," he said.

His idea was to go round asking people if they'd seen a ghost. Then, if it was local, we'd check it out and he'd apply his scientific mind to proving that it was a load of twaddle. We asked lots of people. Three said they didn't believe in ghosts. Debbie Carter thought she'd heard some ghostly footsteps once. Quite a few knew someone else who'd seen a ghost. But there was nothing to go on.

"What did I tell you? Just a load of stupid stories," said Ali.

I wasn't going to argue. If there were any ghosts, I didn't want to go looking for them.

We reached old Mr Fiddy's house. He was sitting in a chair in his strip of front garden, writing. Mr Fiddy had come into school the term before, when we were doing the Second World War in history. He'd talked about serving on the submarines. It was deadly dangerous and really interesting.

Ali leant over the gate.

"Hey, Mr Fiddy! It's us!"

Mr Fiddy looked up. "So it is," he said.

"Mr Fiddy, did you ever see a ghost?"

He put down his pen and looked thoughtful.

"I had a very strange experience once. A long time ago," he said at last. "Whether it was a ghost or not, I couldn't say."

He went back to his writing pad.

I asked if it was when he was on the submarines.

"No – before then. A good deal more frightening too," he said.

Ali's face lit up. He glanced at me, then said, "Could you tell us about it, Mr Fiddy?"

If only he hadn't asked that. If only Mr Fiddy hadn't been sitting outside that day. If only . . . But it's too late for all those 'if's now.

Mr Fiddy got up and said he had things to do. But Ali went on and on. So he said he'd tell us about it if we did a few jobs for him. He wanted some things lifted down from the top of a cupboard. He said he couldn't reach up these days. He had trouble bending too, so he took us to his back garden and pointed out the weeds he wanted pulling up. Then he told us his story.

It happened when he was about sixteen, he said. He and his two mates, Ted and Harry, had cycled over to the big fair on Barton Common.

"It was dark when we cycled back," he told us. "Another ten minutes, we'd have been home. All of a sudden, the skies opened – torrential it was. So we ran for cover – there was an old wreck of a place off the road – and waited for it to ease off a bit. Well, I must have dozed off. Next thing I knew, Harry was shaking me, yelling we had to get out. He was scared witless. The rain had stopped. There was a bit of a moon too. But now the place was icy cold. I could hear muttering. It was Ted, sitting bolt upright against the wall, like he was talking in his sleep. He was staring at the doorway. So I looked. And there was someone – or *something* – standing there . . ."

Mr Fiddy gave a little shiver. "Nothing much more than a shadow. It gave me the shakes, no mistake. I could feel it watching us. Worse than that – a feeling of something bad. I wanted to run, but nothing would have made me go near that doorway. And all the while, Ted was muttering these numbers. Lists of numbers. Six – six – forty-four, six – six – forty-four, and so on. Others too. I froze to the spot. Shut my eyes and chanted the Lord's Prayer, over and over. I don't know how long we sat there. But the cold lifted and I knew the thing had gone. Harry and I grabbed Ted and scarpered. I've never pedalled so fast in all my life. I've not felt terror like that before or since. Strange thing was, Ted couldn't remember any of it. Never believed us. Thought we were pulling his leg."

Mr Fiddy sat staring straight ahead as if he was seeing it all again. Then he pointed at a weed. "You've missed one there."

"Is that it?" said Ali. He sounded disappointed.

"Not quite," said Mr Fiddy.

We waited.

"Go and have a look at the war memorial. You'll

see Ted's name there: Edward Mapes. He was killed in the D-Day landings. Nineteen forty-four, June the sixth."

I didn't get it straight away. But Ali did.

"Six, six, forty-four," he said slowly. "So the numbers were a date – the date Ted was going to die."

"You've got it," said Mr Fiddy. "Makes you think, doesn't it?"

Ali leant forward.

"Mr Fiddy, you said there were other numbers . . ."

Mr Fiddy nodded.

"Do you remember them?"

"Can't ever forget them."

"And?"

"Twenty-five, eleven, eighty-six. And I know what you're going to ask. The answer is, yes. Harry – he was my best man you know – died in his sleep. Twenty-fifth of November, nineteen eighty-six. Heart failure."

"What about . . .?" said Ali. But he didn't finish. He looked a bit embarrassed.

Mr Fiddy gave a stiff smile.

"It's all right. I know what you're getting at. You mean have my numbers come up yet? We'll have to see, won't we?" he sighed. "Now off you go, it's time for my dinner."

"If only we knew where this place was," said Ali as we walked back home. "Then we could check it out."

"You must be kidding," I told him.

"Mr Fiddy's old," he said. "Old people get confused. Their memories get mixed up."

Next day Ali came round again.

"I know where it is!" he cried, as I opened the front door. He was excited and out of breath, holding his bike.

"Where what is, Ali?"

"Where Mr Fiddy and Ted and Harry sheltered from the rain!"

"*What?*"

"It's on Low Road, past the old gravel pit. I timed it – ten minutes by bike, just like Mr Fiddy said. You can see some old chimneys behind the trees – of course the trees would've grown a bit since then."

I blinked at Ali. His scientific research was getting too serious for me. But I was curious.

"What? You went *inside*?" I asked.

"Not yet," he smiled, as if he were saving it up, like a present to be opened.

"It can't be the same place, Ali. For starters, Low Road doesn't lead to Barton Common."

"It used to," Ali said, dropping his bike and

27

taking out a map from his pocket. "See?" he pointed. "Before they built the bypass and cut it off, Low Road was the only way. There's nothing else along that stretch of road. So, this is what we do. Tonight we'll camp out in your tent. Then, when your mum and dad have gone to bed, we sneak off –"

"No way, Ali!" I interrupted. "Absolutely no way!"

Ali turned up that evening with his bike and his sleeping bag. And reinforcements: Shaun and his bike.

"You're mad," I told him. "But OK, you can sleep here. Just don't expect *me* to come along. I don't want to know when I'm going to die. Even in the cause of scientific research."

"Die? As in dead?" piped Shaun, looking alarmed.

Ali hadn't told Shaun about Mr Fiddy's story. So I filled him in.

"Include me out," he groaned when I'd finished. "Are you nuts, Ali?"

Ali shook his head. "It's you two who are nuts, believing in ghosts. OK, Shaun's daft enough to believe anything. But you, Kenny, you've got more sense."

"Better daft than dead," Shaun muttered.

"It's no good going on my own," Ali went on, ignoring Shaun. "I need witnesses. It won't be a proper scientific investigation without witnesses. OK, it might be a bit scary, out there, alone in the dark. But only if you let your imagination run away. You've got to take control of it. Nothing will happen, I promise. Come on! See it as an adventure!"

Shaun and I shook our heads slowly.

"Wimps! Total wimps!" Ali sneered, unrolling his sleeping bag. He grabbed his notebook and pen from his rucksack, wrote something, then got into his bag and turned his back on us.

It got boring after that, playing noughts and crosses and hangman with Shaun.

The next thing I knew was Ali's watch bleeping and his torch flicking on. I squinted at my watch. Twelve thirty-three. I nudged Shaun awake.

Ali leant over. "Your last chance for the adventure of a lifetime," he whispered.

"Or your last adventure, full stop," I said.

"Well, thanks for nothing! Great mates you are!" Ali snapped.

"We'll be the rescue party," I joked. "If you're not back by dawn, we'll come and search for your body." But I couldn't really believe that he'd be daft enough to go.

"Look, I'm telling you. It'll be all right," Ali pleaded.

"Go then, if you're so sure," came a muffled voice from Shaun's sleeping bag.

Ali didn't move. And I realised he wasn't quite as fearless as he made out.

"You're scared," I said slowly. "Go on, admit it, Ali! You're scared."

Ali's torch clicked off.

"Yeah, he's chicken," came Shaun's voice from the darkness. "Just like us. Chick-chick-chicken!" he squawked.

Ali's torch clicked on again, dazzling me.

"OK," he said quietly. "We'll see who's right, shall we?"

He tugged on his trainers, grabbed his torch and left.

"He's kidding," I said.

"Yeah, he'll be back," said Shaun.

We waited. For fifteen minutes we waited. It seemed longer. Perhaps he was there already. It was no good. I couldn't just lie there. Imagining what might be happening was almost as bad as being there myself. I searched for my trainers.

"I'm going after him, Shaun."

"What? You're not leaving me on my own!"

So we both went.

Ali hadn't got very far, as it turned out. We found him inside the bus shelter. He said he was reserving his energy. I knew he'd lost his bottle. But he wouldn't admit it. He never gives in, Ali.

"OK, Ali," I pleaded. "You're not scared. So let's go home and get some sleep, can we?"

He stared down at his feet. "It's just a matter of controlling the imagination," he muttered, like he was reminding himself. "Testing myself is all part of the investigation." He looked up. "You don't have to come." But there was a hopeful look on his face.

"OK, Ali," I sighed. "Just to get it over with, eh?"

"No way, no way," Shaun bleated. But he was scared of going back on his own, so he came too.

We pedalled towards Low Road. At least there was a decent moon. It was as quiet and as still as a grave. Who'd ever find us out here? I was thinking. We should have left a note. We must be crazy.

Ali pointed at the dark outline of two chimneys above some trees. We turned off, keeping close together, bumping over the rough, damp grass. In the bikes' headlights, the twigs looked like claws . . .

Suddenly, there it was: the old house. Walls jagged where the roof had caved in. Great black holes for windows. And a gaping doorway. I remembered Mr Fiddy's story and felt sick. Compared to this place, the faceless ghost seemed quite friendly.

"I don't like it, I don't like it," Shaun stammered.

"Just in and out, Ali," I croaked. "No hanging about."

We shone our torches into the doorway. Shaun didn't have one.

"Ready, steady, go!" I cried.

We ran. Inside our torches seemed to make the dark corners even more menacing.

"Three, eight, ninety-seven," moaned Ali, but his voice was shaky.

It wasn't funny. It was tomorrow's date.

"I've had enough – I'm going," Shaun bleated.

He turned. And stopped. He was staring at something. Something in the doorway. I could see it too. A dark shape that filled the opening, blocking our escape. The air had suddenly become freezing.

"Ali!" I yelled.

Ali didn't seem to hear. He too was staring at the door. Then his torch went out. Shaun started to whimper.

"Run!" I screamed. Then my torch went out too.

I could hear muttering. It was Ali again. "Seventeen, eleven . . ." he droned.

"NO!" I begged. "Cover your ears, Shaun! Cover your ears!"

I plunged my fingers into my ears. The blackness seemed to swallow me. I could sense the closeness of something. Something terrible. I couldn't think or breathe or move. I was rigid with terror. Trapped. Helpless. And my head screaming, "NO! PLEASE! NO!"

How long was I standing there, screaming inside my head? Ten minutes? Ten seconds? I don't know.

Suddenly, a blinding glare. I covered my eyes. A voice boomed . . .

"It's all right, it's all right! It's me!"

It was Mr Fiddy.

I admit it, I was nearly crying by then. Shaun was too. And shivering. We couldn't stop shivering. Ali was stiff, just staring at Mr Fiddy. Our torches were working again.

"What d'you think you're playing at? You foolish boys! Don't you have any sense? Coming out here on your own! Thought it was you I saw go past the house. Go on! I'll follow. Get home! Now!"

We bedded down in my room that night, huddled close together, with the light on. Every time I closed my eyes, I could see that dark shadow and feel the terror.

I still felt shaky next morning. Shaun, staring up at the ceiling from his sleeping bag, looked ill.

And do you know what Ali said? "Pity Mr Fiddy

had to turn up. Didn't have long enough, did we?"

"*What?*" Shaun and I cried together in disbelief.

"Long enough to be terrorised out of my mind!" I spluttered.

"That's what imagination does," Ali said.

"Imagination! Get lost, Ali!" said Shaun. "You were doing a whole lot of shaking last night."

"Just let my imagination go too far. Only briefly though. Next time I won't."

Next time? I couldn't believe what I was hearing. Imagination doesn't put torches out. Imagination doesn't make the temperature drop.

"What about those numbers you were chanting, then?" said Shaun.

"Get real," Ali sighed. "I was winding you up. A joke, Shaun! You never did have much sense of humour."

"He means the second lot of numbers, Ali," I said. "After the torches went out."

"What are you talking about? The torches didn't go out," Ali said.

I swallowed and looked at Shaun. He groaned.

"Ali?" I asked. "How long d'you reckon it was before Mr Fiddy turned up?"

He shrugged. "Thirty seconds?"

"Oh help," shuddered Shaun. "He doesn't remember. Just like Ted in Mr Fiddy's story!"

"Now you're definitely winding me up," said Ali.

"Didn't you see that shadow-thing in the doorway?" Shaun blurted.

"Ha-ha! Very funny!" mocked Ali.

So we told Ali what we'd seen and heard. He didn't believe a word we told him. He insisted he'd been proved right. Nothing had happened – except in our imaginations. I gave up trying, I didn't want to think about it. We'd been stupid. I was feeling bad about old Mr Fiddy too, following us all that way out and back again in the dark. And I needed to talk to him.

"I'm going to Mr Fiddy's," I said, getting up. "See if he's OK."

"What about breakfast?" complained Ali.

I'd lost my appetite. So had Shaun. But they both decided to come with me.

There was no answer when we knocked. We went back a bit later and knocked again.

"It's no good knocking, boys." It was the lady next door to Mr Fiddy. "I'm afraid Mr Fiddy has passed away."

"Passed away where?" asked Shaun.

"He died," she explained. "Very peacefully, in his armchair. That's where I found him."

I couldn't speak. Mr Fiddy was dead. Worse than that. *We'd* killed him. He'd come through the war, the submarines, everything. But we'd finished him off. Made him walk all that way to the ruin and back again. Just made it back home. Collapsed in his chair. And died. We'd murdered him.

I could tell from Ali's and Shaun's faces that they were thinking it too.

"Didn't I see you round here the other day?" the lady asked me.

"Er . . . yeah. We were doing some jobs for him."

She folded her arms. "The funny thing is," she went on, "it's as if he knew. Everything was so tidy. All his things laid out ready on the table. Letters to his son and daughter. His will. A tin with all his important documents . . ."

"What?" I said. "A biscuit tin? With a coach and horses on the lid?"

"How did you know that?" she asked.

"I got it down for him. From the cupboard."

"I thought he was having a nap at first," she said. "So I didn't disturb him. But when I looked in again later, he was still there. Doctor said he probably passed on at about six o'clock."

"Six o'clock this morning?" said Ali.

"No – yesterday evening," she said.

Ali looked as if he'd seen a ghost. He had. We all had. Mr Fiddy's ghost.

"Are you sure?" Ali gulped.

"I know it must be a bit of a shock," she said.

"He was a nice man, Mr Fiddy."

We went and sat on the school wall.

"He didn't look like a ghost," said Shaun.

"He was wearing his old jacket and cap," I said.

"I could smell his cigarettes," said Ali.

It was the first time I'd seen Ali lost for words. He held his head in his hands.

"Tell me again what happened at the old house," he said quietly.

We told him.

"Seventeen, eleven?" he repeated, white-faced. "Those were the numbers? That's all you heard? Not the year?"

We shook our heads.

"Thank goodness for that," he groaned.

"Explain all that *scientifically*, Ali," I said. "If you can."

Life in the Back Row

ANNIE FOX

Sheila had always liked being the shortest girl in her class at Ashing Primary School. Year after year, there she'd be, right in the middle of the front row of the class photograph, holding the sign saying the teacher's name and the class year, while the tall children were all stuck in the back row craning their necks, trying to make sure they got in the photo at all. She was brilliant at gymnastics and when she did make a mistake doing a tumble on the mat, she didn't have far to fall. And quite frankly, because she was so small everyone forgot how old she really was and seemed amazed that she could do anything at all, let alone read and write and do perfectly adequate sums. So, even though she was patted on her blonde head a little more than she would have liked, her size worked for her and all was good.

Until her tenth summer, when her mother said, "Sheila, stop rolling up the waistband on your skirt."

"Yuck," added her brother Jack for good measure.

"I'm not," insisted Sheila, lifting up her shirt-tails to show her mum.

"But it's so short. Maybe it shrank in the wash."

Sheila tried on another of her skirts, and then another and another. All had suddenly become micro-minis. And her trousers were now pedal-pushers. And her shorts were . . . unwearable.

"How could this have happened . . . ? " her mother murmured. Then she announced "To the airing cupboard!"

So Sheila and Jack and Sheila's little sister Kim and their cat trooped to the upstairs airing cupboard where the family height chart was taped inside the cupboard door. Kim began to throw a tantrum so they measured her first. She had grown two centimetres since May. Jack pushed in and fluffed up his dark curly hair for extra height, but was only one centimetre taller. The cat hadn't grown at all. But Sheila . . . Well, Sheila had grown ten centimetres. Or as her mother, who still hadn't fully gone metric, exclaimed, "That's more than four inches!"

Sheila's mother gave her a long, assessing look, then shook her head. "How could I have missed this? You've probably needed new clothes for months!" Sheila could see that her mother was feeling guilty again. She'd recently gone back to full-time work and that made her feel that everything was her fault. "I should have noticed that you were eating more lately."

"Like a pig," Jack added helpfully.

"And you've been getting so tired."

"Yeah, a lazy pig," contributed Jack. "Ow!" He rubbed his shin where Sheila had kicked him. "A *strong* lazy pig," he muttered.

"These are all things that happen when you have a growth spurt," concluded Sheila's mother.

Sheila's mother pulled out the family album and pointed out that although Grandpa Jennings was a little dumpling of a man, Grandma Jennings loomed over him, if not by a head and shoulders, at least by a sharp chin and beaky nose.

"I suppose it could be hereditary," sighed Sheila's mother.

Grandma Jennings! Sheila had vague memories of a stern, elderly woman who bossed everyone around while her pudgy husband smiled benignly. Sheila stared hard at the photograph. Grandma Jennings' hair was drawn back into a severe bun and her lips were pressed firmly together. Is that what I'm going to look like? thought Sheila. What fun that'll be.

"Sheila is a She-Hulk!" shouted Jack.

Sheila not only looked different, she also felt different. She found it harder to judge distances and her aching legs bore a bruise map that charted every table and chair she had collided with. When she sat watching TV, she could no longer tuck her legs neatly under her. Instead, she found herself draping her long limbs over chairs, cushions, sofas as she tried to get comfortable.

But worse was yet to come.

Sheila had been really looking forward to school starting in September. She'd be assembly leader again, she'd probably be the star of the gymnastics team's show, and best of all, she'd see her best friend, Abigail. Like Sheila, Abigail had always been little and blonde and sporty and popular. Maybe not quite as little, blonde, sporty and popular as Sheila was, but near enough. Since Year One, when they had been cast as Angel One (Sheila) and Angel Two (Abigail) in the nativity play, they had been inseparable. Until this summer, when Abigail had gone to visit relatives overseas and they hadn't seen one another for weeks. Would Abigail notice that Sheila had changed? Or maybe Abigail was different now too.

On her first day back at school, Sheila dressed with extra care in her new two-sizes-bigger school clothes. She examined herself in the mirror from every angle. Maybe she wouldn't look too tall if she just bent her knees a bit. No, she still looked big. She tried hunching her shoulders. That made her look a bit shorter. Then she tilted her head. That might do it. She picked up her school bag and went

downstairs, knees bent, hunchbacked and chin to chest. No-one would think she was tall at all. Weird maybe, but not tall. Three steps from the bottom, she tripped over Jack's satchel.

"I was looking for that!" shouted Jack, grabbing his satchel. "Hey! Great forward roll, She-Hulk."

"I need my car keys!" cried Sheila's mother, stepping over Sheila.

"I need my PE kit!" said Jack.

"I need a new life," thought Sheila, as she picked herself up from a heap on the floor.

The class was already queuing up to go into assembly when Sheila, breathless, arrived in the classroom. All the usual crowd of suspects were there. Milly Davenport had a new orthodontic retainer that she was clicking in and out of her mouth to make people giggle. Sam Caseman had his arm in plaster – again. Daniel Stopten, the most obnoxious boy in the class, was doing an annoying airy whistle to himself.

Sheila broke into a huge grin when she saw her best friend Abigail standing, blonde bob shining, at the front of the queue. She rushed over and gave Abigail a hug. But it felt different from before. Abigail's nose just reached Sheila's chin and she was aware of Abigail's startled gaze.

"Sheila?" Abigail said quizzically.

Before Sheila could speak, Mrs Reilly called the class to order. Without thinking, Sheila took her place at the front of the line to lead the class to assembly, as she had always done.

"Er, Sheila, you know we like the students in each class to line up in order of height so that the smallest can sit at the front of hall and get a better view?" her teacher inquired.

"Yes, Mrs Reilly."

"Then whatever are you doing?"

Sheila heard stifled giggles from behind her. She looked round and saw that she was towering above most of her classmates.

"Let's find a more . . . appropriate place for you," said Mrs Reilly, leading Sheila to the end of the queue behind Daniel Stopten. He had an unpleasant smirk on his face as he turned to look at Sheila.

She glared at him. "Don't you dare say a word," she whispered. For once her wishes were obeyed. Daniel just shook his head and did his airy whistle. Great. All year she was going to be stuck sitting next to someone who sounded like an asthmatic budgie.

It was even worse after school at gymnastics. Sheila's mother had replaced most of Sheila's wardrobe but had forgotten about her gymnastics leotard. Sheila did her best to squeeze into it. The sleeves ended somewhere above her elbows and she could only just make the waistband of her tights reach her waist. During the warm-up, as the other gymnasts lightly skipped around the hall, Sheila awkwardly gallumphed around tugging at her tights.

Mrs Olaf, the flamboyant ginger-haired coach, clapped her hands. "Gather round, girls. I have some rather exciting news for you all." The young gymnasts flocked around a beaming Mrs Olaf. "Our team has had the special honour of being chosen to represent our town in the Borough Championships." The girls all applauded and cheered. "And . . . " continued Mrs Olaf holding up one hand. "We will be presenting a gala performance in the school hall at the end of the month. So let's make sure we can do something really stupendous for them. Practice makes . . ."

"Perfect!" the gymnasts shouted.

'Perfectly awful' was how Sheila felt as she watched the other gymnasts run off to do their apparatus work.

"All right, everyone, let's start with the vault!" exclaimed Mrs Olaf. The vault had always been Sheila's speciality, but today she viewed it with trepidation. How would she get any lift-off from those long gangly legs of hers? She watched as the other girls effortlessly floated over the vaulting horse. Abigail, in particular, seemed to fly through the air.

"Well done, Abigail!" cheered Mrs Olaf. "Smashing! I can see you really practised a lot this summer." Abigail blushed with pleasure. Sheila hid in the back of a group pretending to do stretches.

"Where's my star? Sheila?"

Sheila bent down pretending to adjust her slippers, but the other girls nudged her forward.

"Sheila! Now, I want to see that vault with a somersault we were perfecting last year."

The room grew silent as Sheila walked out to the edge of the mat. She stared hard at the vaulting horse. It was simple, really. Wasn't it? Just a run, jump, hands on the vaulting-horse, quick little somersault. Land. Her hands grew moist at the thought of it.

"Go on, Sheila," Abigail said encouragingly. "You can do it."

Sheila took a deep breath and ran down the mat. As she ran, her legs seemed to grow weak beneath her and the room became a blur. She tried to jump, but managed only a little hop. Her damp hands clutched at the vaulting horse, but she slipped and crashed to the floor.

"Are you all right?" fussed Mrs Olaf.

"Just fine," whispered Sheila.

Someone began to giggle.

"All right, girls. Let's try our floor routines . . ."

Abigail came over and offered her a hand up,

but Sheila just shook her head.

"You mustn't give up," Mrs Olaf exclaimed. "Practice makes . . ."

But Sheila just limped away. As the other gymnasts got changed, Sheila sat weeping on a bench, pulling at her tiny leotard. Abigail came over and put her hand on Sheila's shoulder, but Sheila shrugged it off and busied herself with her shoes.

"Do you want to come to my house for tea?" asked Abigail. "I've got so many photos of my holiday to show you."

"Not today," said Sheila. "Thanks." Abigail looked hurt and walked slowly away.

Mrs Olaf sat down beside Sheila. "This isn't like you, Sheila. What happened today?"

"I don't know. I just can't do anything any more," sobbed Sheila.

"Don't be so hard on yourself! We all have the occasional off day."

"An off day! I'm lucky I didn't end up in casualty. My arms and legs just don't go where they're meant to any more."

"You have grown a little bit."

"A little bit? I'm huge!"

"Nonsense!" said Mrs Olaf. "It's just affected your centre of gravity, that's all. Besides, it's nice to be tall. I wish I was."

I know what she's going to say: "Look at all

those models. They're tall", thought Sheila. That's what adults always said. Her mother had been saying it for the past fortnight, to which her brother would always add, "She'd be perfect if you wanted someone to model paper bags."

"Look at all those models . . ." began Mrs Olaf.

"I know, I know," said Sheila miserably. "But what about the gymnastics show? How can I be in it, if I can't do anything?"

"I'm sure we can find some little thing for you to do," said Mrs Olaf. "You have such presence. I know! The perfect thing . . . why don't you stand at the microphone and announce the routines . . .?"

Announce the routines! Sheila fled the hall, vowing never to return to gymnastics club.

After that day, everything changed for Sheila. She sat quietly and miserably at the back of the classroom. At playtimes, she found that the friends she used to look up to she now looked down on. That didn't feel right, so she kept a bit apart from everyone else. Abigail tried to approach her, but they both felt embarrassed to be together. They no longer sat together, so there was no chance to whisper jokes or pass notes. There was less and less for them to share. Abigail seemed to think only about gymnastics and Sheila could only think about her own problems. She would look at Abigail and wonder, had she ever been so aggravatingly perfect and self-assured – and short – as Abigail seemed to her now?

At home, she listened to music, played with her baby sister Kim or – and this was a new pleasure for her – she read. She particularly enjoyed reading books about people who had had hard lives: *The Railway Children, Little Women, The Big Friendly Giant* . . . And she slept. How she slept! "Apparently, Grandma Jennings slept for almost an entire year when she was having her growth spurt," she heard her mother whispering to her auntie on the telephone.

One way or another, Sheila got through each day, but a particular dark cloud was looming – the gymnastics show.

There was a frenzy of activity at Ashing Primary School as everyone prepared for the gala performance. That meant *everyone*. Abigail, who was rapidly promoted to 'star gymnast', would of course perform her perfectly wonderful routine, Sheila reflected sourly. Milly Davenport was beavering away making rosettes. Despite his broken arm, Sam Caseman spent hours designing a striking poster. He'd worked so hard, no-one had the heart to tell him that gymnastics didn't start with a 'J'. Sheila's mother had agreed to make a cake –

though Sheila knew she would end up buying one and trying to pass it off as home-made. Even Sheila's brother Jack was going to appear – as a member of the band, playing his clarinet. "Can I help it if I've got star quality?" he kept saying over breakfast.

Sheila could hardly be more miserable. She suspected Mrs Olaf still thought that she might be persuaded to do the narration for the event. Whenever she saw Mrs Olaf, Sheila quickly ducked out of sight. No way was she going to stand in front of the school announcing "And now Tammy Wing is going to thrill us all by doing a handstand followed by a back flip." Sheila would rather spend a day listening to Jack practise 'Greensleeves' on the clarinet than have anything to do with that stupid show.

"I know what you could do," Jack panted one evening as he was doing some sit-ups in the front room. "They could wrap you – twenty-two – in crêpe paper streamers and pretend – twenty-three – you were a maypole for the gymnasts – twenty-four – to dance around." Sheila restrained herself from reminding Jack that she could still pack a wallop.

The day before the show, Sheila sat on a bench during playtime reading a book. Abigail broke off from skipping rope and came over to join her. Perfect, thought Sheila, she probably wants to brag about how brilliantly she's getting on. Sheila kept her nose in her book.

"Hi," said Abigail shyly.

"Hi." Sheila barely glanced at her. There was a long pause. Abigail took a big breath.

"There's a really good film on TV tonight. Would you like to come over and watch it with me?"

"I don't think so."

"Why not?"

Sheila shrugged and went back to her book. "I've got homework." Not looking up she added, "Besides, you probably want to rest tonight."

"Why?"

"To be fresh for the big show."

"Oh, that . . ."

"And, of course, you have to practise a lot."

Abigail brightened. "Yes, I do."

"Good for you."

Abigail blushed and looked down at her lap. "Are you coming to see it?"

"No."

"I thought you might want to."

"Why?" cried Sheila. "So I can feel really good about all the time I wasted?"

"I thought you might want to see it for my sake," Abigail shot back.

"But it should have been me up there!" cried Sheila.

"Why should it always be you? Not everything is about you, Sheila. You're not the centre of the universe."

That hurt. "I didn't say I was."

"If you were my friend, you'd be happy for me."

"I am," said Sheila weakly as Abigail strode away. But she knew it wasn't true. For years, Abigail had been second best while Sheila got all the praise. Finally Abigail had found something she was the best at. And what had Sheila done? Sulked and resented her. Sheila had been so taken up with feeling like a freak, she realised that she hadn't thought about anyone else's feelings for a long time. She watched Abigail talking animatedly now to Milly Davenport. Milly was probably a better friend to Abigail then she'd ever been. Suddenly, Sheila felt ashamed. That afternoon, when Mrs Reilly asked for volunteers to decorate the school hall for the show, Sheila's was the first hand to go up.

All was not calm in the school hall. The volunteers were being organised by an increasingly anxious Mrs Olaf. "I want all the blue balloons in clusters of three and tied with a white ribbon." She paused. "Or do I mean the other way round?" The students awaited her decision. "Or perhaps white balloons with white ribbons?" Sheila was amazed to see the usually confident Mrs Olaf defeated by the prospect of decorating a school hall. "Or maybe . . ." Mrs Olaf began again.

Mrs Reilly led Mrs Olaf away. "Just make the hall look beautiful," she said over her shoulder.

"It's so nice to know she's totally in control." Daniel Stopten smiled at Sheila.

"Mrs Olaf?" giggled Sheila. "Absolutely calm and collected."

"Since we've got the height advantage, we'd better be in charge of hanging the streamers. Hmmmm, let's do the white ones first . . . no, the blue, no the white, no the blue, let's toss a coin . . ."

Sheila grinned. She grabbed a roll of blue crêpe paper and threw it to Daniel.

"Not bad," he said. "Can you do this?" He ran his long lolloping run down the hall and threw the roll into the basketball hoop. Unravelling as it descended, it shimmered briefly in the air like a blue waterfall.

"I'll try," said Sheila, grabbing up a white roll of crêpe streamers. She dashed up to the hoop, and a white cascade of paper fluttered and fell through it.

Sheila threw her head back and laughed. For the first time in weeks, she felt happy. Why had she always disliked Daniel so much?

"Now try this," said Daniel, scooping up three rolls of streamers. He raised them over his head and took aim.

"Daniel Stopten, what do you think you're doing?" an outraged voice from the back of the hall exclaimed. Mrs Reilly had returned to the hall and was puce with fury. "We asked you here to help decorate the hall, not destroy it."

"It was my fault," Sheila quickly put in. "I had this idea that the basketball hoops would look nice with streamers hanging off them. Daniel was just helping me."

Mrs Reilly looked at Sheila suspiciously but let them get on with the decorations. When they had finished, the hall was a fantasy in blue and white.

Sheila's mother had taken the afternoon off from work to hear Jack play in the band. She gave Sheila a little wave and took a seat near the front, while Sheila headed for the back row.

Daniel slid into the seat next to her. "Basketball team tryouts are next week. I think you should go."

"I don't know," she smiled. "Maybe."

The show was fantastic. Most fantastic of all was Abigail, who tumbled and twisted and balanced and bounded to the huge appreciation of the audience. Sheila felt a shimmer of envy. Could she have ever been that good? Would she ever be good at anything again? But one step at a time, at least she had managed to get through the afternoon without bumping into anything – that was a triumph in itself. She'd been there to cheer an old friend. And maybe she'd made a new one ... The only humiliating moment for her was when Jack decided to show off while the band was playing. He held one note longer and louder than everyone else and ended up squeaking. "Meant to do that," he said loud enough for everyone to hear.

Afterwards, Sheila ran up to congratulate Abigail. When they hugged, it was still awkward, with Sheila's chin practically resting on the top of Abigail's head, but it didn't matter. It felt good.

Mrs Olaf put her hand on Sheila's shoulder. "Wasn't it marvellous?" she beamed. "You know, Sheila, you should have been up there. I'd love you to still be on the team. I never meant you to leave."

"Thank you, Mrs Olaf," Sheila said, "but I don't think I'll have time." Who knows, she thought, I might go up for basketball this year.

"Hey there, She-Hulk!" shouted Jack. Or judo, thought Sheila.

"I'm so proud of you." Sheila's mum had come up behind her and given her a hug.

"Why? I didn't do anything," said Sheila. "Except not fall off my chair."

"I know it wasn't easy for you, watching the show today. And I'm also proud of you for not teasing Jack."

"What do you mean?"

"Sheila, you must have noticed. He's by far the shortest boy in his class. I'm afraid *he* takes after Grandpa Jennings."

Sheila watched her brother across the hall. He did look a bit squat. One of his classmates shouted, "Hey, nice playing, Cube Boy." Jack forced a laugh, but then turned away and caught her eye. Now Sheila knew why he was quick to call her names – look at what he was putting up with at school. Sheila smiled wryly to herself. She'd just been too obsessed with her own problems to notice Jack's. Now that she thought about it, she could think of a few choice names for him too. Where should she begin? Well, let's see, there's . . . But when she saw Jack walking towards them looking small and vulnerable, she knew in that second she wasn't going to use any of them.

Sheila ruffled Jack's hair. "I'm starving," he said.

Sheila's mother locked arms with Jack and Sheila. "Come on. I'm treating both of my stars to a pizza."

"Do you miss gymnastics?" Sheila's mum asked her as they walked down the street.

"A bit," admitted Sheila.

"You know what Grandma Jennings used to say," said her mum.

"What?"

"As one door closes, another opens. Nothing

56

got her down for long. You're like that too."

"Oh, puh-leeze," said Jack.

So that year, in the school photograph it was Abigail who was sitting centre front holding the sign with Mrs Reilly's name on it. Sheila was in the back row, along with Daniel Stopten and the other tall ones, craning her neck to be seen. But no-one could miss Sheila's smile.

That's the Name of the Game

J. BURCHETT AND S. VOGLER

Jim Bright sat in casualty. He wished he was invisible. Everyone was staring. Jim could hear sniggers, but the sniggerers weren't staring at him. They were gawping at the man next to him. Jim wished he had a large notice saying, 'I do not know this man'. The trouble was, he did know him. The man was Jim's dad – and he had a saucepan stuck on his head.

It had started on the fateful morning when Jim woke to find his feet sticking over the end of his mattress.

"Dad, I need a new bed."

As he said it, Jim wished he'd kept his big mouth shut. He could see the ghastly glimmer in his father's eye.

Jim's dad worked at the dump. It didn't pay much, so it was a problem finding money for new football boots, let alone a new bed. But Jim's dad thought of himself as a handy sort of bloke.

"Recycling – that's the name of the game," he would tell Jim at least once a day. He was always

bringing things home from work. Once it was buckled bits of pipe to make a goal for football practice. They were so buckled you could score a goal from behind the shed, at night, with your eyes closed. Then it was a garden gate made of something that looked like asbestos. Most people who came to the house now climbed over the wall instead. And, last week, the shelves – bits of old floorboard. They lasted for a good five minutes. Until his dad proudly put the last saucepan on top.

Yes indeed, Jim wished he'd kept his big mouth shut. His father had the look again.

"A new bed," he said with glee. "You know we've got no money, but don't worry, son." He put his arm round Jim's shoulders. "Recycling – that's the name of the game."

"Yes, Dad," said Jim doubtfully.

Jim heard no more for a while. He hoped his dad had forgotten about the bed. He decided not to complain about sleeping curled up – and he could paint over the lamb and teddy on the headboard before his friend Martin said anything about them at school.

For the next few evenings Jim's dad was very busy. He brought home bulging bin-liners full of milk cartons. "I've had a brilliant idea," he said happily, as he washed them. The cartons put Jim's mind at rest. Dad must have some other crazy scheme on the go. Perhaps it was overtime – a clean-up campaign at the dump.

Then one afternoon Jim pushed open his bedroom door. He stopped dead. The lamb and teddy had gone. Jim's Postman Pat duvet unfortunately hadn't, but it was now lying on a proper bed. "Wow!" he shouted, throwing himself onto his new mattress. "Ow!" he yelled as his back hit something hard.

Dad was standing in the doorway.

"What do you think?" he asked. "I got the idea from those individually sprung mattresses on the advert." He patted the bed lovingly. "You'll have no back trouble with this," he said.

"But I didn't anyway," Jim protested, rubbing his spine. "Till now."

"Nice and firm," his dad went on. "And do you know the best thing about it? It didn't cost a penny."

The awful truth began to dawn.

"You made me a bed from old milk cartons," Jim said.

His dad nodded. "Two hundred and eighty-eight of the little beauties."

Jim decided that a bed of nails would be more comfortable. He didn't like to mention it. With the help of five blankets and a sleeping bag, he got used to the firmness of Dad's 'posture springing'.

Three mornings later, his dad came in to wake him. "Cor, Jim," he said. "Don't you ever change your socks? Smells like something's crawled under your bed and died."

But the smell wasn't coming from under the bed. It *was* the bed. Dad shook his head in disbelief. "That's strange," he said. "I washed those cartons very thoroughly."

So Jim slept on the floor. He quite liked it.

One night Jim and Martin sat watching television. Jim found it difficult to concentrate with the sound of clicking in his ear and his dad muttering. "In, round, through, off. In, round, through, off."

Dad had salvaged a bag of wool from the dump. He was teaching himself to knit. Jim wished his dad hadn't chosen to start when Martin was round. And he wished his dad wouldn't stick his tongue out when he was concentrating. Jim could see Martin watching. He wondered what Martin would say at school. Oh well, he'd be ready for them. He'd stick up for his father. His father didn't waste his time down the pub every night. His dad tried to make the home nice. He did his best – Jim knew that.

And Jim tried hard to remember it when he was

presented with New Bed Mark Two. It was a hammock. It was a stripy hammock – red, purple and orange – with baby blue at the ends. It was a knitted hammock.

"And it didn't cost a penny, did it, Dad?" said Jim. He hoped he looked impressed.

"I knew you'd like it," said his father. "Recycling – that's the name of the game."

To Jim's astonishment, he found the hammock very comfortable. It was slung across a corner of his room. It gave him space underneath to put his things. That night, installed in his hammock, Jim swung gently from side to side. Dad had actually got something right. Jim was proud of him. His mates would be dead jealous. It was really cool to have a hammock.

Jim fell asleep surrounded by dream-loads of admiring friends. When he woke in the morning, he thought he was a lobster trapped in a net, on top of another lobster. Something was digging into his back. He sat up and found himself on a football boot, a snorkel and a stegosaurus. In the night, the wool had stretched.

"Oh well," said his dad. "At least I've taught myself to knit . . . You know, something more solid is called for here."

Jim fought his way out of his woolly cocoon. This sounded more hopeful. His dad went on. "I saw an old car seat at work. You know, the sort that folds down . . ."

Something inside Jim's head exploded. "No!" he screamed. "One false move and I'd be sandwiched. I've got a tool kit. I'll make a bed – with wood."

"Nonsense, son," said Jim's dad. "Do you want people talking about us? You'll have a proper bed – and not just any old bed. Recycling . . ." he began.

"That's the name of the game," muttered Jim. He marched out to the shed – in his pyjamas.

Jim missed the nail and hit his thumb. He had already whacked his ear with the hammer and dropped his Jobsons Junior mallet on his toe. He cast a critical eye over his construction. It looked like a hutch for a giant rabbit. But he had finished the frame. He was pleased with himself. With his tongue stuck out in concentration, he started sawing a piece of wood for the legs. He thought he looked rather professional, like someone on the telly.

"If I want a really expert job," he said to an imaginary camera, "I always use Jobsons Junior Joiner's Kit. And d'you know, Bright's Budget Bed hasn't cost me a penny. Recycling – that's the name of the . . ."

He stopped, horrified. He looked like a boy who

has bitten into an apple and found half a maggot. He flung the saw down and ran gibbering to the house. "I sound like Dad," he panted. "I'm turning into my father!"

As he reached the back door, he could hear his dad banging about in the kitchen, whistling happily. "If he's got that car seat, I'm leaving home!"

Jim kicked the door open and rushed in. To his great relief, Dad was only putting the floorboards back on the wall. "I've found some great glue," he told Jim. "It would take a rampaging elephant to dislodge these shelves."

Dad had the glue in an old saucepan. He put it up on the top shelf. Jim waited for the crash. Nothing happened.

"I want to keep this handy," said his dad. "You never know when I might need it. Well, time for lunch." He stared at Jim. "I'm getting worried about you, son. Why are you still in your pyjamas?"

"Listen, Dad," said Jim, later. "Forget the bed. I don't want a bed. I'll sleep on a lilo or something."

His dad grabbed his arm. He had 'the look'.

"You know, you've got something there, Jim. I'm sure there are a couple of ripped airbeds out in the shed. I could stick 'em together. I could make one lovely big mattress for you. I knew I'd need that glue again."

That evening Jim lowered himself cautiously onto his new bed. The mattress wobbled underneath him. Dad was grinning. "How does it feel?"

"Bit unusual," said Jim.

"Well it would do. I've filled it with water. You've got a water bed there."

That night Jim dreamt he was floating on the Mediterranean. Queen Victoria and Robbie Fowler rowed past in a wheelbarrow.

"Coo-ee!" called Queen Victoria. "We have something for you, young man."

Robbie Fowler threw him a football. "I've signed it," he said.

Jim caught the ball. It was heavy. He began to sink under its weight but he couldn't let go of it.

"Football – that's the name of the game," shouted Queen Victoria. "Take a throw-on."

"We are not amused," said Fowler.

Jim felt the waves lapping over him. He saw his father surfing along on a floorboard. As he sank, he passed an octopus knitting a fin-warmer for a friend. He hit the ocean floor and woke up. He was lying on a piece of flabby rubber in a huge pool of water.

"Dad!" he shouted. "DAD!"

His father stumbled in, rubbing his eyes. "Where's your bed gone?" he asked stupidly.

"I've eaten it, of course!" snapped Jim.

Dad looked at the flat lilo. He looked at his damp slippers. He sprang into action. "You mop it up son. I'll go and see if it's gone through the kitchen ceiling."

Jim heard his father squelching downstairs. Then there was a loud bang, a very rude word and a sort of plop.

Sitting in casualty, Jim wished a friendly hole would open and swallow him up. The nurses had managed to get the pot off Dad's head. Now he sat there, his hair sticking up, stiff with glue. He looked like an electrocuted hedgehog. He was telling the whole story at the top of his voice to a woman who had just come in. The waiting room had gone very quiet.

". . . The water must have dripped down the flex," he explained. "When I switched the kitchen light on, the whole thing blew. Next thing I knew, I was sitting under a pile of shelves with the saucepan stuck on my head." He turned to Jim. "My beautiful shelves," he sighed.

Jim felt sorry for his dad. He was looking miserable. But at least it would put an end to all the nonsense. They'd have to go and buy a bed like ordinary people did.

A doctor poked her head round a door. "Mr Bright?" she said. Sadly and with great dignity, Jim's father stood up. But halfway across the waiting room, he stopped. He was standing in front of a drinks machine. It had a sign: 'Out of Order'. He whipped a tape measure out of his dressing-gown pocket. A slow smile spread over his face.

"I've got it this time, Jim," he called. "I've really got it. You'll love this one, son. A bed *and* a cup of tea in the morning, all in one. What do you think? Jim?. . . JIM!"

'That's the Name of the Game' was broadcast on BBC Radio 4 in January 1996 as one of the winning stories in the 1995 Good Housekeeping/Children's BBC Radio 4 Short Story Competition.

Leopard

RICHARD BROWN

Will woke with a sense that something was wrong. There was a strange sound like a distant growling, then a whisper. It wasn't the whisper of a voice, more like something sleek moving through tall grass.

There was a faint glow in his room too and it wasn't coming from the window. He sat up, rubbing his eyes. His computer was switched on. That was odd, he always switched it off before going to bed. He got up and sat in front of it.

On the screen there was a picture of a leopard – or rather, two pictures. The top one showed the animal moving stealthily through grass, crouched low. In the bottom picture, the leopard was leaping at a terrified man, its claws extended, its fangs sharp and vicious. The caption read: *Leopards are famous for their stealth and agility. They move so silently, they can pounce on a man without a sound . . .*

Will had always been fascinated by these shy, sleek, powerful animals. He touched the screen; it crackled slightly. He traced the outline of the top leopard, then the bottom one. It left a strange feeling in his finger.

Will shivered and got back into bed. He stared at the mysterious leopard until his eyes closed. As he drifted off to sleep, he heard once more the soft growling and the whisper of footfalls in the long grass . . .

"Dad," said Will, sitting at the breakfast table. "Did you turn on my computer last night? That disk on animals?" One glance from Dad was enough. Mum was in the kitchen; he knew better than to ask her 'such a silly question'.

He poured some Sugar Puffs into his bowl; inevitably, some missed and scattered on the table. In trying to pick them up and reach for the milk at the same time, he knocked over the milk carton.

"Not again," said Dad with a sigh. He and Will watched the milk dribble from the milk carton onto the breakfast table. Silently, he fetched a kitchen cloth and mopped up the milk. Dad shook his head, a faint, sceptical smile on his face. He'd got used to his son always making a mess.

Tossing the cloth back into the sink, Will narrowly missed knocking a wine glass off the draining-board. It wobbled precariously. Will's Mum shot out a hand and caught it. "Will!" she shouted. "How many times . . . ?"

But Will was already running upstairs. He tripped twice.

He looked at the computer screen. Surely the tree behind the leopard had been on the left last night? And wasn't the animal closer to the man now?

He moved his hand to switch off the machine. Then, catching the look in the leopard's eye, he changed his mind.

Coming down the stairs, he placed each foot carefully and, this time, he did not stumble once.

He was old enough to walk to school on his own; it was only a mile away. But Mum usually walked across the field at the back of the house with him. She would lean on the gate on the other side of the field and watch him walk down the lane. She had got used to the fact that he never turned to wave to her; he always seemed to be in a world of his own.

"Just try and be a bit more careful," she was saying as they walked down the garden path. Even as she was saying this, Will's foot had somehow managed to stray beyond the edge of the path and ...

"Look out!" Mum shouted.

Too late. The red tulip was already squashed. Mum raised her eyebrows in exaggerated disbelief. Will sighed to himself; he couldn't help it, he'd always been clumsy.

As they walked along the edge of the muddy field path, Will kept his gaze fixed on the ground. He was fearful of tripping over a tuft of grass or treading in cow dung. Suddenly, he saw large pawprints in the mud. He crouched and stared at them. A tingling sensation ran up the back of his neck and over his scalp. "Look, Mum," he said, pointing at the row of pawprints in the mud. They trailed along the path as far as he could see.

"Hmm," Mum said. "Probably made by a Doberman. Or a Great Dane. Though I haven't seen any of those around here, I must say."

Will was hardly listening. On impulse, he placed the fingers of one hand into a pawprint. Then he did the same with the other hand. Something clicked in his mind. He blinked and looked up. It was as if a mist had cleared. Every blade of grass, every dandelion and daisy, even the flies on a dried cowpat, were crystal clear, standing alone, reflecting light. Will stared in astonishment. It was as if he had never really *seen* these things before.

"Will, come on!" he heard Mum call faintly.

Reluctantly, he stood up. As his fingers left the pawprints, the light faded.

He took a few steps towards Mum; but it was as if he could not quite control his feet. Without thinking, he placed one foot in a pawprint, then did the same with the other. Everything around him became intensely bright, solid; every sound found a separate place in his mind.

"Get a move on, Will. I don't know what's got into you today."

Will stepped from pawprint to pawprint. He heard the sound of breathing and felt cold breath on the back of his neck. Turning, he glimpsed what he thought was the misty outline of a . . .

A hand grasped his sleeve. "Will," Mum said, shaking him impatiently. "Stop daydreaming. You'll be late for school."

Walking into the classroom after lunch, Will saw with dismay that the paints had been laid out on the desks. How long would it be before he had knocked over the paint palette? How long before the paint was all over his hands and had found its way to all those bits his painting shirt didn't cover? Even now, in his mind's eye, he could see dark water dripping through soggy newspaper into his desk . . .

And worse: Mrs Matthews had put Michael Fisher next to him.

"No arguing, you two," she warned, wagging her finger at them.

She gathered the painting group around her and showed them a picture called *Tropical Storm with a Tiger*. A jungle of reds, greens and browns was being swept by a gale. Half hidden in the grass, stalking a hunter, was a tiger, its teeth bared, a wild look in its eyes. They were to paint a picture in the same style, a jungle and a wild animal. "Think of a fierce wind," Mrs Matthews urged them cheerfully, "so that everything looks wild and windswept."

Will wasn't good at painting, but he liked the idea of the long waving leaves, the outstretched branches, the gashes of red and orange. Ignoring Fisher, who was grinning at him curiously, he began to mix colours in his palette. Hovering at the back of his mind was the leopard he'd seen on his computer.

Fisher watched him for a while, then he laughed to himself mischievously.

Gradually Will became aware that every time he dipped his brush in paint, mixed a colour or made a mark on the paper, Fisher did exactly the same a fraction of a second later. He stopped in annoyance and glanced at Fisher's picture. It was the same as his own.

"Stop copying me!" Will shouted angrily. His paintbrush jerked back and forth, and from it drops of paint splattered all over Fisher's painting.

Fisher was triumphant. He let out a loud wail, attracting Mrs Matthew's attention.

She cut short Will's protest and ticked him off. "Are you as clumsy as this at home?" she demanded. "Or do you do it on purpose?"

Will went silent.

Fisher was moved away from Will; that at least was something.

But his resentment smouldered. Why did Fisher always pick on him?

In his jungle he painted a leopard rearing up, claws sinking into the body of a boy. The boy was wearing a number eleven football shirt. It just so happened that Fisher was also wearing a number eleven football shirt.

The class soon spread the word. Suddenly, Will was very popular. There was a lot of laughing at Fisher's expense.

When Fisher saw the picture, he drew a sharp breath and curled his fingers into hard fists. "I'll get you for this, Hayward," he threatened. "After school."

Will knew he meant it.

He managed to get out of school first and started to run home. He imagined that he was the leopard in his painting, light, springy, fast. Not once did he trip or lose his balance. Once inside the field, he leant against the gate until his heart stopped thumping.

It was very quiet.

He searched along the muddy path until he found pawprints that had not been spoilt by people walking along the path during the day. Carefully, he placed each of his feet into a pawprint.

His mind clicked again. Once more, everything was sharply in focus, amazingly clear. He moved in awe along the path, slowly stepping from one pawprint to another. He heard every whisper of the breeze, every insect buzzing loudly or whirring wings, every blade of grass rubbing against another.

The light shining through the leaves of a solitary tree dappled his body. Claws edged from his fingers . . .

"Oi, Hayward!"

He stopped. His tail swished back and forth.

There was a thumping of feet behind him. "I said I'd get you," Fisher shouted triumphantly. "Stay where you are!"

Will turned, careful to keep his feet in the pawprints. He made a noise in his throat like a growl.

"Scared, are you?" Fisher sneered. He was only a few metres away now.

Will lifted his paw and bared his claws. He hissed loudly.

At the same moment Fisher stepped by accident into another pair of pawprints. His eyes widened, his jaw dropped, a cry choked in his throat. *Will had gone. In his place not three metres away was – a leopard? But it couldn't be . . .*

As he stumbled backwards in terror, his feet left the pawprints. The leopard faded before his eyes.

There was Will again, his arms upraised, his lips a snarl.

Will was about to leap on Fisher when they were both disturbed by a cry across the field from Will's house. "Will?" It was his mother. "What are you doing?"

Fisher broke free and ran towards Will's mum, panic-stricken. "Mrs Hayward," he blurted out. "It's Will."

"What is it? What's happening?" she demanded, alarmed.

"I don't know. I thought I saw a huge cat . . . like a leopard . . . but . . ."

Mum stared at him in amazement. What was the boy talking about?

Will was now loping through the long grass, his head low, his feet treading lightly, carefully. He moved swiftly to a clump of bushes and crouched behind them.

Mrs Hayward called to her husband, who was working in the garden. "It's Will," she said. "Something's happened to him."

They all ran back into the field and looked around frantically for signs of the boy.

Fisher led them to the pawprints and said, "I saw it here." The Haywards heard the fear in his voice and saw the way his hand shook. They began to search, calling Will's name across the empty field.

They found him crouching behind the bushes. He was twitching slightly, a strange look in his eyes. He hardly seemed to hear them. When Mum approached him, he lashed out. She jumped back in alarm. Dad shouted at him. Will backed away. Dad went in and pinned Will's arms to his side. There was a brief struggle and then the boy went limp.

They carried him out of the field.

Fisher followed them to the garden gate but they seemed to have forgotten him. As he ran off home, he thought, "I'd better keep clear of Hayward. He's crazy."

In the garden, Will became himself again. His parents asked him what he was playing at but he could only shake his head. He hardly knew himself.

That night he dreamt he was walking through his own painting. The wind was whipping the leaves and bushes and wild flowers all around him, but he remained untouched. He prowled, his paws pressing lightly on the ground, disturbing nothing.

He woke with the leopard-feeling still inside him. He buttoned his shirt and buckled his belt without fumbling. His feet hardly touched the stair carpet. At the breakfast table he spilt nothing. He broke nothing in the kitchen. He kept looking at his hands, feet, legs, arms, in growing disbelief and delight. He left for school on time, a gleam of something wild in his eyes.

At school, Fisher kept his distance. Playfully, Will growled at him, moving his hand like a paw back and forth in front of Fisher's pale face.

Will was untouchable. In the playground he balanced on the lines painted on the tarmac without once falling off. He moved more skilfully than anyone on the football field and no-one could get the ball off him. When two boys, jealous of his new prowess, started to threaten him, one glare, one defiant word, was enough to make them back off. His friends watched him with increasing amazement. At lunch time, someone knocked a plastic drinks bottle off the dinner table. Will scooped it up before it had time to reach the ground. He held it up triumphantly.

Back in the field after school, Will was dismayed to see that the daily traffic of people and dogs across the field had obliterated the pawprints. There was nothing in the mud he could now clearly identify as a leopard's mark. He walked back and forth across the field thinking, this new feeling inside me, this new me, the one that fights like a leopard and never puts a foot wrong, will it disappear now?

He ran over to the clump of bushes where he had hidden the day before. Inside, just where he had crouched, he found a tuft of yellow fur hanging from a twig. He unsnagged it and smoothed it out. This was proof.

He took it home and showed Dad.

"Sheep's wool, probably," said Dad, "though it's a bit tough."

"Dog's hair, I'd say," said Mum.

Will took it up to his room. The leopard was still there on the screen. The colour of the fur was the same as his little tuft – well, almost. *Leopards are famous for their stealth and agility* . . . He knotted some string around the tuft and hung it round his neck.

He touched the leopard on the screen. "Thanks," he said. "I'll be all right now," and he switched off the computer. There was a faint after-image of the leopard on the grey screen, like a ghost. Then it was gone.

The Tooth Person

J. BURCHETT AND S. VOGLER

Edward didn't mind that he hadn't lost any of his baby teeth. He didn't mind, even though most of his friends were shedding teeth like cartoon characters in a fight. He didn't even mind that his dog, Fang, had already lost one. His mum said it was good to hang on to your teeth. His dad said it was because they were so healthy. His dentist said everything was fine. The dinner ladies said he had a lovely smile. And Edward believed them. He took every opportunity to flash his perfect teeth. "I don't believe in the tooth fairy anyway," he would say. "It's sissy."

His friends couldn't care less. They were too busy collecting the cash.

One night, Edward was having his usual dream. He had scored a famous penalty. Premier League managers were fighting to sign him up. The press photographers were falling over each other's lenses. And Edward was flashing his smile.

"Ted! Over here!" they were shouting. "Look this way, Ted!"

Edward wanted to fast-forward the dream to

where he was reading the newspaper headlines: 'Ted the Teeth Takes Tottenham to the Top!' He loved this bit. But tonight the photographers wouldn't get off the pitch.

"Ted! Ted!" they kept calling. "Edward!"

He woke up. There was a creature sitting on his pillow. She was dressed in a sugar-pink tracksuit. She wore a tinselly Alice-band. She had tiny silver trainers on her feet and wispy wings on her back.

Yuck! thought Edward.

A large satchel was slung over her shoulder. It said, 'Tooth Express'.

"At last," she lisped. "I thought you'd never wake up."

"What?. . . Who are you?" he asked.

"I'm a tooth fairy, silly," she simpered.

"Tooth fairy? But you don't exist. And anyway I haven't lost any teeth. Look." He gave her the smile.

"That's why I'm here – *because* you haven't lost any teeth. You're perfect. You're going to be very important. You're going to be a Tooth Person."

"Don't know what you're talking about. I'm going back to sleep. I shouldn't have had that fifth banana at teatime. Bad dream, that's what you are."

He banged his head down on the pillow. The tooth fairy bounced off backwards. Edward tried to return to his dream. The fairy scrambled back up the bedclothes. She whacked him over the head.

"Here's your bag," she said sweetly. "Your silver coins, your alarm clock and your magic travelling slippers. Now, where did I put your pink tracksuit?"

Edward looked at the bag, the coins, the clock and the slippers. He pinched himself. It hurt. He must be awake. He knew he wouldn't like the answer but he had to ask. "Why do I need these?"

"Ooh, you are a silly." Edward cringed at her twinkly laugh. "You're the new tooth person. There aren't many children of your age who still have all their first teeth. You should be proud!"

"Hang on," said Edward. "You want me to collect children's teeth and put money under their pillow? Why aren't you fairies doing it? And I'm not wearing a pink tracksuit."

"Not children's teeth," she giggled. "*Fairy* teeth. Our teeth fall out too. Who do you think collects them? A tooth person, of course. And you are the new tooth person until you lose your first tooth. It's simple. You take the tooth from under the fairy's pillow and leave a coin there instead. The uniform is a pink tracksuit. Some people would give anything to have one."

She vanished in a puff of pink glitter.

So Edward became a tooth person. He had no choice. The first time the alarm clock rang, he ignored it and went back to sleep. He found himself flung out of bed. The slippers appeared on his feet and the bag landed round his neck. Worst of all, he was wearing the pink tracksuit.

Then he felt a dreadful sensation. He was shrinking. He whizzed round the room like a deflating balloon. There was an embarrassing noise as well. He landed with a plop on the carpet. But it wasn't his carpet. It wasn't even his own bedroom. A fairy was asleep in a wee trundle bed. Edward had no idea what a wee trundle bed was, but he was sure this was one. The fairy's wings gently quivered as she snored. The scene made him want to be sick. But he knew that the sooner he'd done his task, the sooner he'd be back in bed. He felt around under the fairy's pillow and found a tiny, pearly tooth. He shoved a coin in its place.

Suddenly he was back in his own bedroom, sitting in his tooth mug, clutching the tooth. "What do I do with this?" he asked himself. He searched inside the satchel and found a gold envelope addressed to 'The Tooth Collection Company'. He put the tooth in it and stuck it back in the satchel. He was beginning to wonder how he would explain things to his mum in the morning. It would be a bit of a shock for her, finding her son only ten centimetres tall. Then suddenly he was being stretched in all directions. There was a ghastly creaking noise and the room seemed to shrink.

In the morning the satchel was empty. "They must have an early post," he grunted.

Every night the alarm clock rang. One night it went off twelve times and Edward didn't get to bed at all. He wondered if the fairies had been having a sponsored tooth-pull.

He began to get dark circles under his eyes. He yawned a lot at school. He was too tired to flash his smile. The dinner ladies told his teacher. His teacher told his mother. His mother told his father. His father told the doctor. The doctor told him to go to bed early.

One night he was faced with a quadruple bunk bed. The little fairy who had lost her tooth slept on the top. Edward clambered up wearily. As he got the tooth, the whole bed swayed. Slowly it began to tip. Edward, bedclothes, fairies – everything came down with an enormous clatter. The four fairies emerged from a pile of pillows, screeching and scratching and whacking each other with their wands. Edward cowered under a duvet.

When the coast was clear, he poked a coin under the nearest pillow. "Sort it out yourselves," he hissed.

Later that night, Edward felt a thump in his ear.

"Edward!" said a gruff voice. There was a fairy on his pillow. There was *nothing* sweet about this one. She prodded him with her wand. It had a boxing glove on the end. She was wearing the regulation pink tracksuit, but it was filthy and had holes in the knees. It had 'Big F' written on it. Her silver trainers were badly scuffed. On her head she wore a dog collar with long vicious studs. Her hair was pink and orange and stuck up. She had a huge safety pin in her ear.

"Now you listen here, boy," she said. She rolled up her sleeves. She had a tattoo: *Peace and Love*. "You caused a right punch-up last night, sunshine," she snarled. "Three broken wings and a bent wand."

"It wasn't my fault. It was the bed," said Edward. "I hurt my bottom."

Big F ignored him. Ted the Teeth tried his famous smile. That didn't work either.

"The Tooth Collection Company has high standards," she went on. "You're in big trouble. Do you un-der-stand?" With each syllable she poked him in the face with her wand.

"Mess it up again and you're on Jewellery Service."

"Jewellery service?"

"Yeah – you know. What do you think we do with all those teeth? We recycle them. We make

earrings, bracelets, that sort of thing. For the little princesses. It's very dainty work and you'll be on the all-night shift or my name's not Felicity Twinkletoes Junior. I can see it now," she smirked. " 'Tottenham Ted Threads Teeth for Tiny Tiaras'."

"No way!" said Edward. He saw the boxing glove twitch. "There's no way I'm going to get it wrong again," he said quickly.

"Just don't forget," she grunted. "Sleep tight. Don't let the bed bugs bite!"

She disappeared.

Edward lay in bed quivering. He couldn't believe it. He'd had the frighteners put on him – by a tooth fairy. He was being bullied by something the size of a potato.

He was sore where Big F had poked him. He felt the gum. One of his teeth was loose! Oh no! The dream, the glory, the headlines, the dinner ladies. He'd lose it all.

"If she's done for Ted the Teeth, I'll stamp on all ten of her twinkletoes," he said.

Then it hit him. His brain lit up like the Blackpool Illuminations. This was his way out! If he lost a tooth, Big F couldn't touch him. He'd be free!

At school next day, Edward watched Sally Robins who had a very loose tooth. She rocked it backwards and forwards with her tongue. Then she twisted it round and round until with great delight, she held the tooth up. "That's my seventh one," she said proudly. "More work for the tooth fairy." Edward flinched.

His tooth was hardly moving. He needed to get it out quickly. He decided to ask around. His friends mocked.

"Need the cash?"

"Don't they like the smile any more?"

"Got an arrangement with the tooth fairy?"

Micky's two front teeth had been knocked out when his mouth had collided with Ruth's head. Edward decided it would be too painful. His friends told him the art of the Wiggle, the Prod and the Twist. Lisa remembered a story her grandad had told her.

"His mother tied a thread around his wobbly tooth and the other end to the door handle. Then she slammed the door shut and the tooth came out." The children groaned.

That evening Edward wiggled. He prodded. His tooth resisted the Twist. He remembered Lisa's story. He stood with his eyes closed, a thread hanging between his tooth and the door handle. He wasn't sure if he could go through with it. Then he remembered Big F. He kicked the door hard.

He felt . . . nothing at all.

"I must be super tough," he thought. "Top strikers always are."

He opened his eyes. The tooth hadn't moved. The thread was too long. He started all over again. He didn't wait this time. He slammed the door. The door hit his father, who was coming in with a cup in his hand.

"What's going on?" shouted Dad. He was sitting in a pool of tea. "I don't know what's got into you lately. An early night – that's what the doctor said."

Edward stomped upstairs. He kicked his school bag across the bedroom. He shouted at Fang who fled. Then the alarm rang. "I haven't even been to bed yet!" he yelled as he began to shrink and whizz round the room.

He felt under the pillow of the sleeping fairy. Something was different. There wasn't a tooth. Instead there was a piece of chalk. He'd been tricked! This was the last straw. He grabbed the chalk and wrote in large letters on the wall:

TOOTH FAIRIES
DON'T MESS WITH
BIG E OR ELSE!

Back in his bedroom, Edward began to sweat. He was in trouble. Big F would be on her way and it wouldn't be for a game of tiddly-winks. He rummaged in his school bag looking for a ruler to fight her off with. All he could find was an apple.

"Edward," came the voice. "You're in it up to your molars, mate." Edward gulped nervously and bit into the apple. To show he wasn't scared, he tried to whistle, but just spat apple all over Big F who had appeared on the carpet.

"I warned you. It's Jewellery Service for you tonight. Eight-hour shifts, five minutes' lunch-break, bring your own sandwiches."

"But I haven't had any sleep," said Edward, feebly.

"Don't argue. Just be there."

Edward took a desperate bite of his apple. It hurt. He tasted blood. He ran his finger along his teeth and suddenly came to a gap. He could feel gum. And there, stuck in the apple, was his tooth. He held it out to Big F and gave her a gruesome, bloodstained grin.

"Ding!" The alarm clock disappeared.

"Zing!" The satchel went.

"Ping!" The slippers and tracksuit were gone.

Big F vanished in a furious explosion of muscles and tattoos.

Edward charged downstairs and burst into the kitchen, frightening his mum and setting Fang off yelping.

"My tooth's come out!" he yelled. "My first tooth."

"Is that all? I thought the house was on fire," said Mum. "Stick it under your pillow for the tooth fairy."

Edward stopped. The nightmare wasn't over. "No!" he shouted. "I'm not letting her anywhere near me!"

He ran out clutching the tooth. Mum turned to Fang. "What's the matter with him?" she asked. "If I didn't know better I'd think he was scared of the tooth fairy."

Edward ran upstairs. Then he ran down again. "I've got to get rid of it. But where?" He looked round wildly. "Down the loo!" he yelled. "She won't want to go after it in there."

He threw the tooth into the toilet and flushed it as hard as he could. When the water stopped bubbling, the tooth popped up again. He pulled the chain ten more times. Each time he thought it had gone. Each time it bobbed back up. "Yuck!" he said, as he fished it out.

I'll stick it in the dustbin, he thought. No, that was no good. It would be sitting there waiting for her.

He began to search desperately round. He found a newspaper. He wrapped the tooth in sheet after sheet. It looked like an enormous 'pass the parcel'.

Just to make sure, he took the sellotape and wound it round and round.

To his mum's astonishment, Edward raced past her into the garden. He thought of kicking the parcel over into next door's garden. But they would only throw it back.

"Edward!"

It sounded like Mum – or was it Big F?

He ran into the shed, got a spade and sprinted to the end of the garden. He began to dig a very deep hole.

Threpperton via Scadge

DENNIS HAMLEY

Michael lived so far away from his school that when the school bus picked him up every morning he was the only passenger all the way to Scadge. He had the bus to himself as it chugged over the moor, along the side of the bluff with the steep gorge on the other side, then down into Scadge village itself. Here the bus filled up with friends – and enemies – and off they all went to the big world, Threpperton and school.

But there was no school bus on Saturday mornings. So if he wanted to play for the school team, Michael had to go on the ordinary service bus and pay. Well, he wanted to, so he did.

Michael knew about buses: Bristols, AECs, Scammells, Leylands, Volvos; coachwork by Plaxton. He loved the great lumbering beasts. Once, he was told, Threpperton Corporation double-deckers ran all the way to this barren spot. No more: instead, little titches, made by Iveco, Renault, Mercedes, sometimes no more than minibuses.

But the destination remained the same: ROUTE 71, THREPPERTON VIA SCADGE. And the time the bus rolled up was the same – and also the fact that Michael would stand at the stop, sports bag at his feet, alone, week after week.

And the bus would be the same as well. A green and cream single-decker Dennis Handybus. Michael liked it. It was quiet, comfortable, modern.

But one Saturday morning, two things were different. First, Michael wasn't alone at the bus stop and second, the vehicle that turned the corner and stopped in front of the pub opposite the entrance to his father's farm was not a Dennis Handybus.

Four other people stood at the bus stop. There was a thin, wiry man wearing a flat cap, big boots and a cowman's smock. There was a fat, red-faced and wheezy woman wearing a dark green coat and carrying a shopping basket. There was a young man with shiny black hair. He wore a blue suit with black velvet facings on the lapels and narrow trousers. He stood arm-in-arm with a girl who had wavy blonde hair and wore a billowy red skirt, white blouse and an incredibly wide, incredibly tight, yellow belt. Michael knew none of them. Odd, that: he thought he knew everybody within a three-mile radius.

And then the bus came round the corner. It wheezed as uncomfortably as the fat woman and shuddered to a halt.

Michael gasped.

It was a double-decker, red with a white roof and a white panel above the windows of the lower deck. And – amazing and wonderful for the true bus expert like Michael – the manufacturer's name, in big silver letters on the grille at the front, was ALBION. He didn't remember ever seeing an Albion before except in a museum.

Well, fair enough. He knew some companies did up old buses in their original colours and put them in service for a bit of publicity. So why not here?

The entrance was at the back. The other four boarded. Michael followed. The driver sat in a cab completely cut off from the passengers: for the first time in his life, Michael would have his ticket issued by a bus conductor.

And there he was, standing at the foot of the stairs. He wore a green uniform and a peaked cap. He stood watching the passengers board. They all walked straight past him – no buying of tickets as they got on. Michael was puzzled, but then, like the others, he passed the conductor and rushed up the stairs. The conductor pressed the bell, and the Albion ground and coughed its way along the road away from the little knot of houses.

The top deck was empty. Michael ran to the front and sat where he had a panoramic view. The bus swayed gently but perceptibly – it was, thought Michael, like being on top of the mast of a sailing ship. He had never seen a double-decker as far out of town as this: from where he was, the bus seemed too wide for the narrow road that wound through the wild, lonely moors.

There were footsteps behind him. "Any more fares, please?" The thin, sallow conductor stood over him.

"Threpperton bus station," said Michael and handed over the exact fare. The man, expressionless, rolled off a ticket from the machine slung round his neck and Michael watched, entranced. Vintage bus travel was all right.

Now the bus was feeling its way downhill, gingerly negotiating the sharp bends round the bluff. One moment, the rocky sides seemed very close to the windows on the right. The next, the bus seemed in danger of clipping the guard-rails on the left. On the Handybus, Michael often watched the driver's deft manoeuvres of the steering wheel during this part of the journey; he noticed the slight squeezes of the brakes and the frequent gear changes. From up here, on the top deck of the Albion, he couldn't see the driver, but he heard the ponderous old engine chug and nearly stop, and felt gear changes rack the whole bus. And from this high vantage point the scene was truly alarming. The bus swayed. The guard-rails looked so puny and the waters of the River Chewn in the gorge below looked so dark, frothy and menacing: suddenly, things were scary.

He was thankful when the bluff, the river and the gorge were left behind and they were moving steadily along the main road into Scadge. Here, Michael looked out for his mates – Ricky and Baz got on here. Several more people boarded: three women with headscarves, one with a large pram which the conductor stowed under the stairs; a man in a fawn mackintosh; another in a duffel coat; and two boys Michael didn't know, who wore red blazers and caps. But Ricky and Baz weren't there.

Michael heard the tramp of footsteps up the stairs: the red-blazered boys came and sat three seats behind him. He turned to look at them; they ignored him. They were reading comics. One had the *Hotspur*, the other, the *Eagle*. They were quietly absorbed.

Michael was worried. Had he got on the wrong bus? The Albion ground its way out of Scadge – and certainly took the right road. The boys both said, "Half single to Threpperton, please," to the conductor when he clumped up the stairs.

Michael shrugged his shoulders. Ricky and Baz? The twerps had missed the bus. How would the team manage without them?

Now they approached a big town. Threpperton. No mistake about it. The Albion nosed its way through the busy streets and finally nudged slowly into the bus station. The old diesel engine ticked and throbbed irregularly as first the red-blazered boys, then Michael, clambered down the stairs.

Outside the bus station, the cold air hit him in the face. The boys seemed to have gone. In front of him stood Ricky and Baz. "Where did you get to?" said Ricky.

As they walked from the bus station to the school, Michael was having difficulty explaining things to Ricky and Baz. "I came on this vintage bus," he said. "An old red Albion. I bet it was fifty years old."

"Don't be daft," said Baz.

"I'm not. It's what they call a heritage bus. They do the same with trains. Do up old ones and make a big thing of it."

"Only because they can't afford new ones," said Ricky.

"Well, maybe. So why shouldn't I have come here on one?"

"But you didn't," said Baz.

"I *did*. I was *on* it."

"Well, why didn't we see it, then?" said Ricky.

It was true. When Michael had met them and turned to demonstrate his remarkable mode of transport, it seemed to have quietly made off.

"Come on, admit it," said Baz. "You were on the

bus and you hid from us. Stupid joke, but that's what you did."

Michael was tired of arguing.

"Yes, you're right," he said. "That's just what I did."

It was a good morning. They played West Park and beat them 5–1. Michael scored. He was pleased with himself as he, Ricky and Baz, sports bags swinging delightedly, ambled back to the bus station. "Stick with us this time," said Ricky. "No hiding," said Baz. No need. The Dennis Handybus stood waiting in its bay at the bus station and the smooth journey home was nothing out of the ordinary.

Michael looked out for the Albion throughout the following week. He never saw it. The next Saturday the school team wasn't playing. He looked at the bus stop at the time he would have caught the bus, had there been a game. No Albion: just the usual Dennis.

But the week after, they were playing Baker's End. Michael stood at the bus stop. With him were the man wearing a flat cap, big boots and a cowman's smock, the fat and wheezy woman and the dark-haired man in the blue suit with his wasp-waisted girlfriend. And, *chug-chug-cough*, round the corner came the red Albion.

"Are you thick or something?" demanded Baz. "It wasn't funny the first time. Twice and it's just plain stupid."

"Don't listen to the idiot," said Ricky.

Of course, part of the reason they were all angry was that Baker's End had won 3–2, Michael had scored an own goal and suddenly the Schools' District League Championship didn't look a foregone conclusion. So Michael was miserable anyway. But more than that – his journey had been just the same as two weeks before, even down to the two silent, red-capped and red-blazered boys reading the *Hotspur* and the *Eagle*. No Ricky and Baz getting on at Scadge. But there they were at Threpperton bus station saying, "You've done it again."

"But . . ." said Michael. Then he shut up. *What* had he done again? Why didn't Ricky and Baz seem to know what he was talking about? It worried him. He hadn't been able to concentrate on the game. "We may as well have a zombie in the team!" Ricky had shouted at him after his own goal.

After Scadge, the journey past the gorge and bluff to home was lonely and depressing. The rest of the day dragged; that night Michael didn't sleep much. The bus he had explained to himself all right – but who were the people? Especially the boys in blazers.

Even though next day was Sunday, Dad was out in the fields with his shepherds. Michael spoke to his mother. "Mum, is there a school round here where boys wear red caps and blazers?" Mum laughed.

"There was," she said. "The one your dad went to. He hated it."

Dad in a blazer? He tried to picture the tough, weatherbeaten face with a red school cap on top. He couldn't.

"The old boys' grammar school in Threpperton. It's gone now, merged with the girls' high school and two secondary moderns years ago. They joined up into the big comprehensive where you'll be next year. There was a terrific row when the grammar school closed. Ask your dad."

When Dad came in for his lunch, Michael did ask him.

"Yes," he said. "That cap and blazer. I looked a real twerp in them. Couldn't wait to get shot of the lot. Funny. When it all went, I was so angry I wrote to the local paper about it." He considered his roast beef and Yorkshire pudding for a moment. "It's strange to see you going off on Saturday mornings to play football and *wanting* to," he said. "I remember we *had* to go to Saturday morning school. Barbaric. Our parents thought it was marvellous. I wouldn't wish it on anyone."

He speared a roast potato. "Strange days," he said. He chewed it and swallowed. "Great days," he added, smiling.

"I bet," said Michael.

So what did it all mean? Who were those two boys in blazers and caps? Who were all the other people on the bus? Michael thought he knew everyone for miles around in that lonely area. Why did nobody else seem to see them? He turned it over and over in his mind and came to no answer at all. What would happen on his next journey, to the match against St Ignatius which would decide the Schools' District League Championship?

On Sunday night it rained. The rain continued through Monday and Tuesday. On Wednesday it eased, but that night it returned, along with bitter, high winds. The River Chewn flooded. Michael's head teacher reported that the pitch at St Ignatius was under half a metre of water. There would be no game on Saturday.

On Friday, the head teacher announced there *would* be a game after all, as a new date couldn't be arranged. The two schools had found some money to hire the all-weather pitch at the local sports centre. "The show must go on," said the head teacher.

So Saturday came and Michael waited at the bus stop in windy drizzle. His four regular companions stood there as well.

"Bit parky this morning," he said to the young man and his girlfriend.

No answer.

He turned to the wheezy woman.

"Rotten weather this week," he said.

She made no sign of having heard him.

The Albion, still wheezing worse than the woman, staggered round the corner and stopped. Michael saw the driver in his cab, hands spread over the huge steering wheel, face intent and unsmiling.

The four passengers boarded; Michael followed. The same sallow conductor waited at the foot of the stairs. Michael passed him, climbed the stairs and went to his usual lonely seat at the front. "Ting-ting," went the bell. The diesel engine gave a little growl as if annoyed at being woken up. Then it howled shakily as the driver engaged first gear and let out the clutch.

Now the Albion crept along in high wind: rattling raindrops flecked the window in front of Michael and he felt the high sides of the bus buffeted by sudden gusts. The pub, houses and farm slowly receded. The open moor beckoned – then the hazardous, bendy drop round the bluff, skirting the edge of the gorge.

The diesel engine was working very hard this morning. The bus shook; the seats juddered.

"Any more fares, please?"

The conductor was there. Michael handed him the exact fare. He didn't even turn to look as he said, "Threpperton bus station, please." He took the ticket automatically and put it in his pocket.

The Albion was negotiating the first of the bends. Michael couldn't take his eyes off the road. He waited for the familiar jerky check of brakes and gear change. But the Albion didn't seem to change speed at all.

A blast of wind blowing straight across the moors and slapping into the side of the bluff seemed to make the bus swerve. Another bend was ahead. The Albion once again did not seem to slow. The shaking increased: the bus rolled in a new gust.

Suddenly Michael was very scared. Another bend: a shudder, almost as if the driver was changing down all the gears to a dead stop. But the Albion still charged on.

Now Michael could see the guard-rails at the side of the road. Deep below in the gorge were the racing, foaming waters of the River Chewn, swollen to twice its size and force by a week of torrential rain.

And now Michael knew.

"The bus is out of control!" he yelled. He snatched up his sports bag, dashed along the gangway and nearly threw himself downstairs.

The conductor stood in his usual place at the foot of the stairs. "THE BUS IS OUT OF CONTROL!" Michael shrieked at him. No answer. Michael saw the head-and-shoulders back view of the passengers who had got on with him. They sat swaying with the movement of the bus.

"THE BUS . . ." he started.

No use. There was nothing else for it. He'd have to jump.

The green verge of the road was moving past in a a blur. He daren't just leap off the bus at that speed. But what else could he do? Something awful was about to happen and he didn't want to be part of it. Taking a deep breath, he let go of the handrail and stepped off into thin air.

He hit the ground with a jarring thud and rolled over and over before lying still. For a moment he couldn't move. Then he shook his head and tried to pick himself up. No bones broken. He had landed in soft bracken. He looked down the road.

The Albion was disappearing away from him not fifty metres away, about to negotiate a bend to the right. But even as he looked, the bus seemed to keep going straight on.

Michael screamed.

"NO! STOP!"

The Albion smashed through the guard-rails and disappeared over the edge of the bluff.

Michael rushed forward. The guard-rails were twisted and flattened as if they had been made of toffee. Twenty metres below in the churning torrent, the Albion was being swept away. It was on its side. White foam washed over it. Nobody could have escaped.

Michael's head was spinning. He felt faint. His feet were heavy as lead. What was he to do?

For a few moments, as he stood alone in the pouring rain, he could not think. This was a hard and rocky place, yet the ground seemed squelchy and muddy. For an instant, he thought the ground moved under his feet, as if giants living far below were shifting in their sleep.

He'd never get to Scadge now, let alone Threpperton. He *had* to reach the nearest people and tell them what had happened.

He found the will to start walking back the way he had just come. His mind was numb with shock as he put one foot slowly in front of the other, rain beating into his face on this lonely road.

No, it wasn't so lonely. A shape loomed up ahead. A vehicle, headlights on in this murky weather, was coming towards him.

The Dennis Handybus.

What was it doing here? The Albion had been running the Saturday morning service.

No matter. Now he could tell people about the accident – and warn them of the broken guard-rail.

Michael jumped into the middle of the road, waving his arms. The Dennis slowed and stopped. The driver got out. "What do you think you're playing at?" she shouted angrily.

"There's been an accident," Michael gabbled. "They've gone over into the river. The guard-rails have gone."

The driver's anger died. "Take me there," she said.

They hurried on together, round the bend to where the guard-rails were broken. But as they approached, Michael's head started spinning again.

The guard-rails were intact. Nothing had touched them.

"But I was on the bus," he stuttered. "And I jumped off. I saw the bus go over the edge."

"You'd better see a doctor, boy," said the driver. "You're either daft or having me on. Either way I don't like it."

"I'm not. I *did* see it happen."

"Come on. I'll take you to Threpperton."

"I've got no money left," Michael said.

Then he felt a jingle in his pocket. The exact

fare to Threpperton. So where was the ticket he'd been given on the Albion? He felt in his pocket again. Nothing. "I don't understand – " he started.

"Come on," said the driver. "I've got a timetable to keep to."

They turned and walked towards the Dennis.

Behind them, there was a sudden rushing, roaring noise. They looked back.

The guard-rail was disappearing before their eyes. A rush of mud and gravel disappeared with it. The road cracked: part of the asphalt moved as well. It was as if a giant had stood up in the gorge, his feet in the river, and bitten a slice out of the bluff like a piece of cake.

"My God," said the driver. "The rain must have weakened the topsoil and the road foundations. If you hadn't stopped me, we'd have gone with it!"

She examined the sliced-off road that was left.

"I can get past this if I take it easy," she said. "We've got to get to Scadge so I can raise the alarm. Come on, get in. It's a free ride for you."

As she sat down behind her wheel she said, "*What* bus did you say you were on?"

"An old Albion."

"Funny," she replied. "There was an Albion that went over the side in weather like this in 1956. Driver, conductor, passengers – all killed – they never had a chance."

She restarted the Dennis and steered it cautiously along the single carriageway that was all that remained of the road. Michael held his breath until the last bend was rounded and they were on the straight and level again.

In Scadge, the driver stopped and went straight to a phone box. Ricky and Baz got on. "Tired of playing silly devils, are we?" said Ricky.

The driver returned. The Dennis started. As they left the bus shelter, Michael could have sworn that for a split second he saw two boys in blue macs, with red caps turned dark maroon by the rain, looking impatiently at their watches. But they vanished.

Soon the bus reached the junction with the main road to Threpperton. The rain stopped and the wind died down.

Michael sat in a daze. Ricky and Baz might as well not have been there. But as they drew near the bus station, he realised he'd had a great escape and now there was a big game to play in. When they reached the all-weather pitch and the rest of the team, he knew he was up to it.

He scored twice as they beat St Ignatius 3–0 and won the Schools' District League Championship. But on the way home, passing the bluff in the Dennis Handybus and seeing again the twisted guard-rail where the road had fallen away, he shuddered at what had happened that morning, and at what might have happened if the ghosts from long ago had not come back to save others from their fate.

FALKIRK COUNCIL
LIBRARY SUPPORT
FOR SCHOOLS